IT'S TIME TO EAT MANDARINS

It's Time to Eat MANDARINS

Walter the Educator

Silent King Books
A WhichHead Entertainment Imprint

Copyright © 2024 by Walter the Educator

All rights reserved. No part of this book may be reproduced in any manner whatsoever without written per- mission except in the case of brief quotations embodied in critical articles and reviews.

First Printing, 2024

Disclaimer

This book is a literary work; the story is not about specific persons, locations, situations, and/or circumstances unless mentioned in a historical context. Any resemblance to real persons, locations, situations, and/or circumstances is coincidental. This book is for entertainment and informational purposes only. The author and publisher offer this information without warranties expressed or implied. No matter the grounds, neither the author nor the publisher will be accountable for any losses, injuries, or other damages caused by the reader's use of this book. The use of this book acknowledges an understanding and acceptance of this disclaimer.

It's Time to Eat MANDARINS is a collectible early learning book by Walter the Educator suitable for all ages belonging to Walter the Educator's Time to Eat Book Series. Collect more books at WaltertheEducator.com

USE THE EXTRA SPACE TO TAKE NOTES AND DOCUMENT YOUR MEMORIES

MANDARINS

It's time to eat, the moment's here,

It's Time to Eat
Mandarin

Mandarins bring us joy and cheer!

Bright and orange, round and sweet,

A little fruit that's fun to eat.

Peel the skin, it's thin and light,

The scent is fresh, the color bright.

Tiny pieces, one by one,

Mandarins make snacking fun!

Hold a segment, take a bite,

Juicy goodness feels just right.

Soft and tangy, oh, so sweet,

Mandarins are a tasty treat!

They fit so nicely in your hand,

A snack from nature, oh so grand.

No need for forks, no need for knives,

Mandarins make our taste buds thrive!

It's Time to Eat Mandarin

Packed with sunshine, full of zest,

This citrus fruit is simply the best.

It keeps you strong, it makes you glow,

Mandarins help you learn and grow!

Share them with your family,

They're perfect for you and me.

Pass them 'round, it's such a treat,

Mandarins make moments sweet.

They come from trees, so big and green,

With shiny leaves that shimmer and gleam.

Mandarins hang like golden treasure,

A gift from nature, beyond all measure.

Take them in your lunch to school,

They'll keep you fresh and feeling cool.

A healthy snack, so good to eat,

It's Time to Eat
Mandarin

Mandarins make life extra sweet.

Peel them quick, or take your time,

Each little piece tastes so divine.

The juice will drip, but that's okay,

Mandarins brighten up your day!

So let's all cheer, the time is right,

Mandarins make our hearts feel light.

A fruit so simple, pure, and true,

It's Time to Eat
Mandarin

It's time to eat, let's share a few!

ABOUT THE CREATOR

Walter the Educator is one of the pseudonyms for Walter Anderson. Formally educated in Chemistry, Business, and Education, he is an educator, an author, a diverse entrepreneur, and he is the son of a disabled war veteran. "Walter the Educator" shares his time between educating and creating. He holds interests and owns several creative projects that entertain, enlighten, enhance, and educate, hoping to inspire and motivate you. Follow, find new works, and stay up to date with Walter the Educator™

at WaltertheEducator.com

www.ingramcontent.com/pod-product-compliance
Lightning Source LLC
LaVergne TN
LVHW010411070526
838199LV00064B/5257